JUJU BUGS

A NEW ORLEANS AND THE NATURAL SIDE OF LOUISIANA NATURALIST COMPANION FOR ALL AGES

JOHN LACARBIERE III

This book is dedicated to every last life force that has led to the creation of this book. I hope that those who hold this book gain a deeper personal connection with nature and self, and that the knowledge they gain from that connection is shared with all those that they love.

Photography By: John Lacarbiere III

Locations:
- City Park
- Audubon Park
- Audubon Louisiana Nature Center
- Audubon Zoo
- Bayou Sauvage
- Big Branch Marsh
- Jean Lafitte National Park
- Bayou Signette
- Lake Ponchatrain
- Mississippi River
- My Backyard
- Fontainebleau State Park
- A Studio in the Woods
- All around New Orleans

A special Thank You to Jalisa Roberts, Natisha Cook, Charleyne Lacarbiere, and Cecelia Evans, who played a major role in making this book happen.

TABLE OF CONTENTS

This Book isn't designed to be read from front to back (although you can). It is meant for you to skip around and find the page that best fits your moment in nature.

Your Name:

____

NATURALLY ORLEANS, 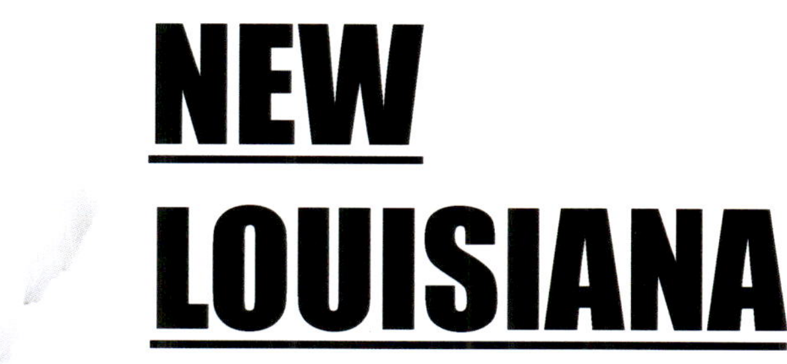 NEW LOUISIANA

My earliest connection with nature that I can remember was maybe 5 or 6 years old playing in my backyard. Behind the tool shed you'd find me digging in the dirt: finding beetles, beetle larvae, earthworms, ants, and so much more, as I opened my eyes to what was my natural world at the time. I remember I would find caterpillars on leaves, put them in jars, and watch them eat and cocoon and eventually become butterflies. I thought the whole process was just so cool. The more time I spent outside, the more I wanted to see. I remember falling in love with City Park and Bayou St. John. Walking the Couturie Forest in City Park, I would see so much wildlife. I would be amazed by all the nutria that would line the bayou at night. In addition to spending time outside, I would read any nature book I could get my hands on and watch every nature show that I could to learn more about the animals I was seeing and the environment they lived in. That eventually led to me becoming a Jr. Zookeeper at the Audubon Zoo here in New Orleans when I was 14. I was able to be hands-on with some of the animals, learn about conservation efforts, and share my knowledge of the animals with the many guests that would come to the zoo. I only worked there for a year, but that experience had me seriously considering becoming a zoologist. I have to thank my mom and my Momo for introducing me to nature in the first place. Be it the walks outside, them allowing me to take care of their plants, or them nurturing my relationship with the outside world, the love they inspired stayed with me into adulthood and that love has not only been something I share, but has been one of my many forms of meditation. Spending time in nature has been good for my mental health and is also good for the planet because everything is connected. This book is created to serve as a companion to help strengthen any naturalist's (of any age) relationship with the outside world, especially (but not limited to) New Orleans. A place I've been in love with since the day I was born Take this with you any time you go outside, even if it's just outside your front door. I promise you will want this with you…

So what is the natural side of Louisiana?

Louisiana is a state rich in natural beauty and biodiversity! From the marshlands of the coast to the bayous of the inland, from the piney woods of the north to the swamps of the south; Louisiana offers a wide range of habitats and ecosystems that are home to a vast array of plants and animals.
This guidebook aims to help you explore and appreciate Louisiana's natural wonders. Whether you are a resident or a visitor, a nature enthusiast or a casual hiker; this book will provide you with useful information, tips, and insights to make the most of your outdoor adventures.

In the following pages, you will find descriptions of some of the most iconic and representative natural areas in Louisiana, as well as practical advice on how to get there, what to see and do, and how to stay safe and responsible. You will also learn about the ecological and cultural significance of these places, and how they are interconnected with the history and identity of Louisiana. But before we dive into the specifics, let's take a moment to appreciate what makes Louisiana's nature so special.

The Diversity of Louisiana's Nature

Louisiana is a state of contrasts and diversity. On one hand, it is famous for its wetlands and swamps, which cover over 40% of its land area and are home to a unique assemblage of plants and animals adapted to the fluctuating water levels and salinity. The Louisiana wetlands are not only a biological hotspot but also a vital economic and cultural resource, providing food, shelter, and recreation for millions of people.

On the other hand, Louisiana also boasts upland forests, prairies, hills, and mountains, which offer different habitats and landscapes to explore. The Kisatchie National Forest in central Louisiana, for example, is one of the largest and most diverse national forests in the South; spanning over 600,000 acres and hosting 11 different plant communities and over 1500 species of plants.
Moreover, Louisiana is a crossroads of ecological zones; blending elements of the temperate, subtropical, and tropical climates. This gives rise to a variety of biotic zones, from the northern hardwoods to the southern cypress swamps, and from the coastal prairies to the Mississippi floodplains.

The Wildlife of Louisiana

The abundance and diversity of Louisiana's natural habitats translate into a rich and fascinating wildlife. Louisiana is home to over 450 species of birds, making it one of the top bird-watching destinations in the country. From the majestic bald eagle to the elusive ivory-billed woodpecker, from the colorful painted bunting to the migratory warblers, Louisiana's avifauna is a sight to behold.

But birds are just the tip of the iceberg. Louisiana also harbors a great variety of mammals, reptiles, amphibians, and fish. The state's waterways are teeming with catfish, bass, crawfish, and alligators, while its forests and fields are inhabited by deer, squirrels, raccoons, and rabbits, among others.

It's worth noting that some of Louisiana's wildlife species are endangered or threatened, due to habitat loss, pollution, and overhunting. As responsible nature lovers, it's our duty to learn about these species and their needs, and to do our part in preserving their habitats and populations.

The Importance of Conservation

Louisiana's nature is not only beautiful and fascinating, but also fragile and threatened. The state's wetlands, in particular, are facing a multitude of challenges: from erosion and subsidence to pollution and climate change. These challenges not only affect the wildlife and habitats of the wetlands, but also the people and communities that depend on them

Underside of a Yellow Garden Spider taken at The Louisiana Nature Center.

This book will take you on a journey through the city of New Orleans and its surrounding areas. You can bring it with you on your walks through City Park. Audubon Park, The Louisiana Nature Center, Jean Lafitte Preserve National Park, Bayou Sauvage, Lafraniere Park, Fountainbleu State Park, The River, The Lake, Irish Bayou, Bayou St. John, and so much more.

What natural areas have you already visited?

____

____

____

THINGS YOU MIGHT NEED

- Comfortable clothing (be sure to check weather before going out)

- Water

- Snacks

- Sun Protection (sunscreen, hats, sunglasses)

- First Aid Kit

- Protective Shoes

- This book

- Insect repellent

- Magnifying glass

- Portable microscope

- Binoculars

- Camera

- Tarp or temporary shelter (tent, sleeping bag)

- Knife

- Walking stick

- Seek app on phone (must be downloaded)

- Identification

- Trash bags

- Map and/or compass

- Something to write or draw with

- Canvas and paint

- Life jacket

5 ESSENTIAL QUESTIONS

Before we get deeper into this book, let's see if we can answer these 5 essential questions to start getting our minds focused on nature. We will revisit them later in the book.

1. Where do you like to spend time in nature?

2. How can nature help you personally?

3. How much time do you spend in nature?

4. How does spending time in nature make you feel?

5. What do you feel your role is in nature?

SAFETY

It's important that when we spend time in nature, we are being safe as well. Here's a few safety tips and things to watch out for.

Animal Homes

When spending time in nature it is important that we're mindful of animal homes. Just like our homes, their homes serve as shelter from weather, a place to rest, hide from predators, raise young, as well as store food. Do not destroy, disrupt, or get too close, because some animals will protect their homes at all cost. Others will abandon their homes (including their children). Binoculars and/or camera lenses are great for closer looks.

- **Stay on designated trails**: Stick to marked paths and avoid going off-trail. This helps protect the local flora and fauna, and prevents you from getting lost.

- **Dress appropriately:** Wear weather-appropriate clothing, including sturdy shoes, sunscreen, and insect repellent. Check the weather forecast before you go and plan accordingly.

- **Bring plenty of water and snacks:** Stay hydrated and keep your energy levels up with enough water and nutritious snacks, especially during hot weather or strenuous hikes.

- **Tell someone your plans:** Let someone know where you're going and when you expect to return. If possible, bring a hiking buddy with you for added safety.

- **Be aware of wildlife:** Respect wildlife by observing from a safe distance and not feeding or approaching them. Keep food securely stored to avoid attracting wildlife to your location.

- **Use caution near water and be mindful of slippery surfaces:** If you're near rivers, lakes, or other bodies of water, be cautious of slippery rocks and currents. Never leave children unattended near water. Rocks, roots, and other natural surfaces can be slippery, especially when wet. Use caution and wear appropriate footwear with good traction to prevent slips and falls.

- **Be cautious of water activities:** If engaging in water activities such as swimming, boating, or kayaking, always wear appropriate safety gear, follow water safety guidelines, and be aware of currents and water conditions.

- **Be prepared for emergencies:** Bring a first aid kit, a map or compass, a whistle, and a fully charged cell phone for emergencies. Know the location of the nearest emergency services.

- **Respect nature and leave no trace:** Leave nature as you found it by not littering and properly disposing of any trash. Follow the *Leave No Trace* principles, which include packing out all trash and minimizing campfire impact.

- **Be mindful of weather conditions:** Keep an eye on weather conditions and be prepared to change your plans if necessary. Avoid hiking during thunderstorms or in extreme weather conditions.

- **Practice sun safety:** Protect yourself from the sun by wearing a hat, sunglasses, and using sunscreen. Take regular breaks in shaded areas to avoid sunburn and heat exhaustion.

- **Be cautious with fire:** If camping or having a campfire, follow all fire regulations and guidelines. Use designated fire rings or fire pits and fully extinguish fires before leaving. Be mindful of fire danger during dry seasons.

- **Avoid poisonous plants:** Learn to identify poisonous plants such as poison ivy, poison oak, and poison sumac, and avoid touching or brushing against them to prevent skin irritation or allergic reactions.

- **Beware of ticks and other insects:** Wear insect repellent to protect against ticks, mosquitoes, and other insects that may carry diseases. Conduct regular tick checks on yourself and others after spending time in wooded or grassy areas.

ECOSYSTEMS

New Orleans and its surrounding areas consists of marshes, swamps, open water, and hardwood forests

Louisiana's geology and landforms have played a crucial role in shaping its ecosystems and supporting a diverse range of wildlife. Here are some ways in which this influence can be seen:

1. **Coastal Wetlands:** Louisiana's coastal wetlands are one of the most productive ecosystems on the planet. They support a rich diversity of fish, shellfish, and other aquatic life, which in turn support a variety of birds and mammals. The wetlands act as a nursery ground for juvenile fish and shellfish, which helps to sustain commercial and recreational fishing industries.

2. **Mississippi River Delta:** The Mississippi River Delta, located in southern Louisiana, is a vast and complex system of interconnected wetlands, estuaries, and barrier islands. This unique ecosystem provides habitat for a wide range of species, including fish, birds, alligators, and various types of vegetation.

3. **Piney Woods:** Louisiana's Piney Woods region is characterized by rolling hills, forests, and grasslands. This area supports a variety of wildlife, including white-tailed deer, wild turkey, and various species of birds.

4. **Atchafalaya Basin:** The Atchafalaya Basin is the largest wetland and swamp in the United States. It is home to numerous species of wildlife, including alligators, otters, and various species of fish and birds.

5. **Salt Domes:** Louisiana's coastal plain contains numerous salt domes, which have been exploited for oil and gas. These domes also support unique ecosystems, with some being home to rare species of plants and animals.

Overall, Louisiana's geology and landforms have played a critical role in shaping its ecosystems and supporting a diverse range of wildlife. However, these ecosystems are also under threat from human activities such as habitat destruction, pollution, and climate change, which highlights the need for continued conservation efforts to protect these important ecosystems and the wildlife they support.

Louisiana's wetlands face a multitude of challenges, some of which are outlined below:

1. **Erosion and Subsidence:** Louisiana's wetlands are prone to erosion and <u>subsidence</u>, which is the sinking or settling of the land. This is due to a combination of factors, including natural processes (such as sediment compaction) as well as human activities (such as oil and gas extraction and the construction of levees). As the wetlands erode and subside, they become more vulnerable to flooding and storm surge, and the habitats they provide for plants and animals are lost.

2. **Pollution:** The wetlands of Louisiana are subject to pollution from various sources, including agricultural runoff, industrial discharges, and urban stormwater runoff. This pollution can harm or kill the plants and animals that live in the wetlands, as well as contaminate the water that people and animals depend on.

3. **Overfishing and Hunting:** Louisiana's wetlands are home to a variety of fish and game species that are important for both ecological and cultural reasons. Overfishing and hunting can deplete populations and disrupt the delicate balance of the wetland ecosystem.

4. **Invasive Species:** Invasive species, such as the nutria (a large rodent originally from South America) can damage wetland habitats by eating the roots of plants and destabilizing the soil.

Invasive species can also outcompete native species for resources, reducing biodiversity and altering the wetland ecosystem.

5.   **Climate Change:** Climate change is affecting Louisiana's wetlands in several ways. Rising sea levels are causing saltwater intrusion into freshwater wetlands, changing the composition of plant and animal communities. Warmer temperatures and changing precipitation patterns are altering the timing and intensity of seasonal cycles, which affects the migration and breeding patterns of wildlife. Extreme weather events (such as hurricanes) are becoming more frequent and intense, causing erosion and damage to wetland habitats.

These are just a few of the challenges facing Louisiana's wetlands. Protecting and restoring these valuable ecosystems requires a multifaceted approach that includes reducing human impacts, monitoring and controlling invasive species, and adapting to the changing climate.

There are several conservation efforts being undertaken in Louisiana to protect and restore its wetlands and other natural resources. Here are some examples:

1.   **Coastal Restoration and Protection:** The Louisiana Coastal Protection and Restoration Authority (CPRA) is responsible for implementing the state's Coastal Master Plan, a comprehensive strategy for restoring and protecting the coast. The plan includes measures such as building new wetlands, restoring barrier islands, and improving coastal infrastructure.

2.   **Habitat Conservation:** The Louisiana Department of Wildlife and Fisheries (LDWF) manages a network of wildlife management areas and refuges throughout the state, providing habitat for a variety of species. The LDWF also works with private landowners to implement habitat conservation practices on their property.

3.   **Invasive Species Management:** The Louisiana Invasive Species Council coordinates efforts to control and manage invasive species in the state, including the nutria and other invasive rodents. The council also works to prevent the introduction of new invasive species.

4.   **Water Quality Improvement:** The Louisiana Department of Environmental Quality (LDEQ) monitors water quality throughout the state and works with industry and municipalities to reduce pollution. The LDEQ also works with farmers to implement conservation practices that reduce agricultural runoff.

5.   **Climate Adaptation:** The Louisiana Office of Community Development manages the state's Hazard Mitigation Grant Program, which provides funding for projects that reduce the risk of damage from natural disasters such as hurricanes and floods. The program also funds projects that help communities adapt to the impacts of climate change.

These are just a few examples of the conservation efforts being undertaken in Louisiana. Effective conservation requires a collaborative approach involving government agencies, non-profit organizations, private landowners, and the public. By working together, we can protect Louisiana's natural resources for future generations.

MINDFULNESS & BREATHING

Stop… take a moment to focus on your breath. Take another to center yourself. Sit down if you need to. Otherwise, stand with your feet about shoulder width apart and relax your knees. Take 5 deep breaths. Inhale through your nose, being sure to fill your belly instead of your chest. Exhale through your mouth, allowing whatever sound that comes to you to come out. But be mindful of what and who's around, because you don't want to be too loud. This is quiet time…

What is Mindfulness?

I like to define mindfulness as a mental state you allow yourself to reach. It brings you to a present moment to hear yourself clearly. It can be a way of experiencing quiet in a loud space, space that allows you to think about how you feel and process those feelings without any response or bias.

Ways Mindfulness Can Be Helpful in Nature

- It helps us focus our attention on whatever the task outside might be.

- It calms us, which is great for those who want to get a little closer to the wildlife for photography.

- It gets us in a healthy habit of breathing.

- It can help us become or feel more connected to the environment.

- It feels good.

Spending time in nature can have a variety of spiritual effects on individuals. Here are some examples:

1. **Increased sense of connectedness:** Many people report feeling a sense of connectedness or oneness with nature when they spend time outdoors. This can foster feelings of awe, wonder, and reverence for the natural world, and may contribute to a deeper sense of purpose or meaning in life.

2. **Improved mental health:** Studies have shown that spending time in nature can have positive effects on mental health, including reducing stress and anxiety, improving mood, and increasing feelings of well-being. These effects may be related to the restorative properties of natural environments, such as the calming sounds of water, the beauty of natural landscapes, and the absence of urban noise and pollution.

3. **Greater sense of mindfulness:** Being in nature can encourage people to be more present and mindful, as they tune into the sights, sounds, and sensations of their surroundings. This can promote a sense of peace and tranquility, and may help individuals develop a greater sense of inner peace and awareness.

4. **Connection to spiritual traditions:** Many spiritual traditions, including Native American and Buddhist traditions, have long recognized the importance of nature in fostering spiritual growth and well-being. Spending time in natural settings can therefore help individuals connect with these traditions and tap into the wisdom and practices they offer.

Overall, spending time in nature can be a powerful tool for spiritual growth, helping individuals cultivate a deeper sense of connection, mindfulness, and well-being.

I Spy With My Little Eye

A fun childhood game that I still play is *"I Spy With My Little Eye."* It is one of my favorite ways to practice mindfulness in nature. It helps me notice things I may have overlooked on other occasions, opening up doors to new discoveries (like discovering the green metallic bees that would pollinate my cucumber flowers in my backyard). Had I not played the game that forces me to pay closer attention, I may have never found that out. I still remember the joy I felt, and that energy carried over and inspired me to create my first ever nature photography book of the same name. Whenever I play, I'm always sure to have my camera with me to capture some of the moments. You can find a nice spot in nature and let things move around you or you can take a nature walk or hike and see as many things as possible as you follow or create your own paths. (The book *I Spy With My Little Eye* is a great companion for this book)

ENDANGERED SPECIES

Louisiana is home to several species that are listed as endangered or threatened under the Endangered Species Act (ESA). Here are a few examples:

1. **Louisiana Black Bear (*Ursus americanus luteolus*):** The Louisiana black bear is a subspecies of the American black bear, and is listed as threatened under the ESA. Habitat loss and hunting are the main threats to the bear's survival.

2. **Red-cockaded Woodpecker**: The red-cockaded woodpecker is a small, non-migratory bird that is listed as endangered under the ESA. Habitat loss and fragmentation are the primary threats to the species.

3. **Whooping Crane:** The whooping crane is a large, migratory bird that is listed as endangered under the ESA. The species was nearly extinct in the 1940s, but conservation efforts have helped to increase the population.

4. **Mississippi Gopher Frog:** The Mississippi gopher frog is a small, aquatic frog that is listed as endangered under the ESA. Habitat loss and degradation are the main threats to the species.

5. **Gulf Sturgeon:** The Gulf sturgeon is a large, prehistoric-looking fish that is listed as threatened under the ESA. Habitat loss, dam construction, and overfishing have all contributed to the species' decline.

6. **Mississippi Gopher Frog (*Lithobates sevosus*)**: This rare frog species is listed as endangered under the U.S. Endangered Species Act. It is found in isolated ponds and wetlands in Mississippi and Louisiana.

7. **Fat Threeridge Mussel (*Amblema neislerii*):** This freshwater mussel species is listed as endangered under the U.S. Endangered Species Act. It is found in certain rivers and streams in Louisiana and Mississippi.

8. **Black Pine Snake (*Pituophis melanoleucus lodingi*):** This subspecies of the eastern pine snake is listed as threatened under the U.S. Endangered Species Act. It is found in sandy areas of Louisiana, Alabama, and Mississippi.

9. **Ringed Map Turtle (*Graptemys oculifera*):** This freshwater turtle species is listed as threatened under the U.S. Endangered Species Act. It is found in certain rivers and bayous in Louisiana, as well as Texas and Mexico.

10. **Pallid Sturgeon (*Scaphirhynchus albus*):** This large, primitive fish species is listed as endangered under the U.S. Endangered Species Act. It is found in the Mississippi River and some of its tributaries, including the Red River in Louisiana.

11. **Louisiana Pearlshell Mussel (*Margaritifera hembeli*):** This freshwater mussel species is listed as endangered under the U.S. Endangered Species Act. It is found in certain rivers and streams in Louisiana and Texas.

12. **Reddish Egret (*Egretta rufescens*):** This bird species is listed as threatened under the U.S. Endangered Species Act. It is found in coastal marshes and wetlands in Louisiana, as well as other Gulf Coast states.

Now that you know about some of these endangered species, how would you like to help?

____
____
____
____
____

This is a photo of the endangered black bear taken at the Audubon Zoo.

STATE FLORA & FAUNA

The state **bird** of Louisiana is the brown pelican (*Pelecanus occidentalis*). The brown pelican is a large, distinctive bird with a long, hooked bill and a wingspan of up to 7 feet. It is known for its dramatic dive-bombing technique to catch fish, which it then stores in its bill pouch to eat later. The brown pelican was designated as the state bird of Louisiana in 1966, and is a common sight along the state's coastal areas, including the barrier islands, wetlands, and beaches.

The state **insect** of Louisiana is the honeybee (*Apis mellifera*). Honeybees play an important role in agriculture by pollinating crops and producing honey, and they are also a vital part of the state's culture and history. Louisiana has a long tradition of beekeeping, with the first honeybees brought to the state by French settlers in the 1700s. The honeybee was designated as the state insect of Louisiana in 1977 to recognize its economic and cultural significance to the state.

The state **reptile** of Louisiana is the alligator (*Alligator mississippiensis*). Alligators are large, semi-aquatic reptiles that are found throughout Louisiana's wetlands, marshes, and swamps. They can grow up to 14 feet in length and can weigh over 1,000 pounds. Alligators are an important part of Louisiana's culture and economy, as they are hunted for their meat and hides. The alligator was designated as the state reptile of Louisiana in 1983.

The state **mammal** of Louisiana is the Louisiana black bear (*Ursus americanus luteolus*). The Louisiana black bear is a subspecies of the American black bear and is found in the state's bottomland hardwood forests and coastal marshes. The Louisiana black bear was once abundant in the region, but habitat loss and overhunting led to a significant decline in the population. The bear was listed as a threatened species in 1992 under the Encangered Species Act. In 1995, the Louisiana black bear was designated as the state mammal of Louisiana to recognize its cultural and ecological importance to the state.

The state **amphibian** of Louisiana is the green tree frog (*Hyla cinerea*). The green tree frog is a small, arboreal frog that is found throughout Louisiana's wetlands, forests, and urban areas. It is known for its bright green color and distinctive call, which sounds like a soft, nasal "quonk-quonk." The green tree frog was designated as the state amphibian of Louisiana in 1993 to recognize its abundance and cultural significance to the state. The frog is often used as a symbol of Louisiana's natural beauty and as a mascot for various sports teams and organizations in the state.

The state **fish** of Louisiana is the white perch (*Morone americana*), also known as the *sac-a-lait* in Cajun French. The white perch is a popular game fish found in Louisiana's lakes, rivers, and bayous. It is known for its delicious, white, flaky meat and is a staple of Cajun and Creole cuisine. The white perch was designated as the state fish of Louisiana in 1993 to recognize its cultural and economic importance to the state.

The state **crustacean** of Louisiana is the Louisiana crawfish (*Procambarus clarkii*). The Louisiana crawfish is a freshwater crustacean that is found in the state's swamps, bayous, and wetlands. It is known for its distinctive red color and is a popular food item in Louisiana, where it is boiled with Cajun spices and served as a delicacy. The Louisiana crawfish was designated as the state crustacean of Louisiana in 1983 to recognize its cultural and economic importance to the state.

The state **mollusk** of Louisiana is the eastern oyster (*Crassostrea virginica*). The eastern oyster is a bivalve mollusk that is found in the state's coastal waters, estuaries, and bays. Oysters are an important part of Louisiana's culture and cuisine, and the state is known for its delicious oyster dishes, such as oyster po'boys and oyster Rockefeller. The eastern oyster was designated as the state mollusk of Louisiana in 2008 to recognize its cultural and economic importance to the state.

The state **tree** of Louisiana is the bald cypress (*Taxodium distichum*). The bald cypress is a large, long-lived tree that is found in Louisiana's wetlands, bayous, and swamps. It is known for its distinctive "knees," which are woody projections that extend above the water level, and for its ability to thrive in waterlogged soil. The bald cypress is an important part of Louisiana's cultural and ecological heritage, and it is used for a variety of purposes, including lumber, mulch, and wildlife habitat. The bald cypress was designated as the state tree of Louisiana in 1963.

The state **flower** of Louisiana is the magnolia (*Magnolia grandiflora*). The magnolia is a large, flowering tree that is found throughout Louisiana, and it is known for its large, fragrant white flowers and glossy evergreen leaves. The magnolia has a long history of cultural and symbolic significance in Louisiana, and it is often used as a decorative element in architecture and design. The magnolia was designated as the state flower of Louisiana in 1900.

The state **plant** of Louisiana is the Louisiana iris (*Iris giganticaerulea*). The Louisiana iris is a flowering plant that is native to Louisiana and the southeastern United States. It is known for its large, showy flowers, which come in a range of colors, including blue, purple, yellow, and white. The Louisiana iris is an important part of Louisiana's cultural and ecological heritage, and it is often used in landscaping and gardening. The Louisiana iris was designated as the state wildflower of Louisiana in 1990.

The state **butterfly** of Louisiana is the Eastern tiger swallowtail (*Papilio glaucus*). This butterfly is native to much of the eastern United States, including Louisiana, and it is known for its large size and striking coloration. The Eastern tiger swallowtail has yellow and black wings with blue and orange markings, and it is often found near rivers, streams, and other bodies of water. It was designated as the state butterfly of Louisiana in 1995 to recognize its beauty and ecological importance to the state.

The state **fossil** of Louisiana is petrified palmwood. Petrified palmwood is a type of fossilized wood that is made up of ancient palm trees that have been preserved over millions of years. It is found in several areas of Louisiana, including the Catahoula Formation and the Cockfield Formation. Petrified palmwood is known for its distinctive patterns and colors, which are created by the replacement of organic materials with minerals over time. It was designated as the state fossil of Louisiana in 1976 to recognize its importance to the state's geology and natural history.

ASTRONOMY IS NATURE

What is your relationship with the sun and the moon?

What is your relationship with the other planets, stars, and other things in space?

Astronomy is the scientific study of celestial objects (such as stars, planets, galaxies, and other objects in the universe) and their interactions and behaviors. Astronomy is considered a part of nature as it seeks to understand the natural phenomena that occur in the vastness of the cosmos.

Astronomy studies the physical properties, compositions, and behaviors of celestial objects using a variety of scientific methods; including observation, measurement, and mathematical modeling. Astronomers use telescopes, spectroscopy, and other instruments to collect data from distant objects, analyze the data, and develop theories and explanations for the observed phenomena.

Astronomy is part of our natural world in several ways:

1. **Celestial objects:** Astronomy studies the diverse range of celestial objects that exist in the universe, such as stars, planets, asteroids, comets, galaxies, and black holes. These objects are part of the natural universe and are subject to the laws of physics and other natural forces.

2. **Natural phenomena:** Astronomy investigates natural phenomena that occur in the universe, such as supernovae, planetary eclipses, gravitational waves, and cosmic rays. These events are part of the natural processes that shape the universe and have a profound impact on its evolution.

3. **Natural laws:** Astronomy seeks to understand and describe the natural laws that govern the behavior and properties of celestial objects, such as gravity, electromagnetism, and thermodynamics. These aws are fundamental principles that govern the behavior of celestial objects and are an essential part of nature.

4. **Interactions with other natural systems:** Astronomy also studies how celestial objects interact with other natural systems, such as the effects of stars on the evolution of galaxies, the gravitational influence of planets on their moons, or the interaction between a comet and a planet's atmosphere. These interactions are part of the natural dynamics that occur in the universe.

So what does all of that have to do with nature walks and spending time in nature?

For me, watching the sun rise and set is extremely calming. Watching the moon and stars for me can be energizing. Mindfully watching the sun and the moon lets me know what time it is. Knowing what time it is lets me know what animals and plants will be out or hiding. Knowing what time it is lets me know the seasons, based on the sun and the moon's positions. Spending time with the celestial bodies helps me get a better understanding of the overall connection of things: how the sun plays a major role in plant photosynthesis, how the moon controls the tides of the ocean, how the moon cycle sometimes dictates life cycles in animals. It's all fascinating to me. I encourage you to watch the sunset and the sunrise. Spend time with the moon in all of its phases. There are several dark areas in Louisiana to catch several stars and their constellations, as well as planets. New Orleans doesn't always have the darkest sky, but if you find yourself near Bayou Savauge and the start of Highway 11, you may forget you're in the city by the way the sky lights up with stars.

NATURE COMPANION SHEETS

With this section, you'll be able to journal, write down your observations and sketch images. If you have the *Seek* app, use it to help Identify species.

Draw an image of something you see

List the things you see on your walk:

Journal: Here, you can write down your experiences in nature. Think about things that happened, moments that stood out, or how you felt during the walk. Who you were with? What animals or plants did you feel a connection to? Think about sounds and smells. Write freely.

With this section, you'll be able to journal, write down your observations and sketch images. If you have the *Seek* app, use it to help Identify species.

<table>
<tr><td>

Draw an image of something you see

</td><td>

List the things you see on your walk:

</td></tr>
</table>

Journal: Here, you can write down your experiences in nature. Think about things that happened, moments that stood out, or how you felt during the walk. Who you were with? What animals or plants did you feel a connection to? Think about sounds and smells. Write freely.

With this section, you'll be able to journal, write down your observations and sketch images. If you have the *Seek* app, use it to help Identify species.

| **Draw an image of something you see** | **List the things you see on your walk:** |

Journal: Here, you can write down your experiences in nature. Think about things that happened, moments that stood out, or how you felt during the walk. Who you were with? What animals or plants did you feel a connection to? Think about sounds and smells. Write freely.

With this section, you'll be able to journal, write down your observations and sketch images. If you have the *Seek* app, use it to help Identify species.

<table>
<tr><td>

Draw an image of something you see

</td><td>

List the things you see on your walk:

</td></tr>
</table>

Journal: Here, you can write down your experiences in nature. Think about things that happened, moments that stood out, or how you felt during the walk. Who you were with? What animals or plants did you feel a connection to? Think about sounds and smells. Write freely.

With this section, you'll be able to journal, write down your observations and sketch images. If you have the *Seek* app, use it to help Identify species.

<table>
<tr><td>

Draw an image of something you see

</td><td>

List the things you see on your walk:

</td></tr>
</table>

Journal: Here, you can write down your experiences in nature. Think about things that happened, moments that stood out, or how you felt during the walk. Who you were with? What animals or plants did you feel a connection to? Think about sounds and smells. Write freely.

With this section, you'll be able to journal, write down your observations and sketch images. If you have the *Seek* app, use it to help Identify species.

Draw an image of something you see

List the things you see on your walk:

Journal: Here, you can write down your experiences in nature. Think about things that happened, moments that stood out, or how you felt during the walk. Who you were with? What animals or plants did you feel a connection to? Think about sounds and smells. Write freely.

With this section, you'll be able to journal, write down your observations and sketch images. If you have the *Seek* app, use it to help Identify species.

<table>
<tr><td>

Draw an image of something you see

</td><td>

List the things you see on your walk:

</td></tr>
</table>

Journal: Here, you can write down your experiences in nature. Think about things that happened, moments that stood out, or how you felt during the walk. Who you were with? What animals or plants did you feel a connection to? Think about sounds and smells. Write freely.

With this section, you'll be able to journal, write down your observations and sketch images. If you have the *Seek* app, use it to help Identify species.

Draw an image of something you see	List the things you see on your walk:

Journal: Here, you can write down your experiences in nature. Think about things that happened, moments that stood out, or how you felt during the walk. Who you were with? What animals or plants did you feel a connection to? Think about sounds and smells. Write freely.

With this section, you'll be able to journal, write down your observations and sketch images. If you have the *Seek* app, use it to help Identify species.

Draw an image of something you see

List the things you see on your walk:

Journal: Here, you can write down your experiences in nature. Think about things that happened, moments that stood out, or how you felt during the walk. Who you were with? What animals or plants did you feel a connection to? Think about sounds and smells. Write freely.

With this section, you'll be able to journal, write down your observations and sketch images. If you have the *Seek* app, use it to help Identify species.

<table>
<tr><td>Draw an image of something you see</td><td>List the things you see on your walk:</td></tr>
</table>

Journal: Here, you can write down your experiences in nature. Think about things that happened, moments that stood out, or how you felt during the walk. Who you were with? What animals or plants did you feel a connection to? Think about sounds and smells. Write freely.

With this section, you'll be able to journal, write down your observations and sketch images. If you have the *Seek* app, use it to help Identify species.

<table>
<tr><td>

Draw an image of something you see

</td><td>

List the things you see on your walk:

</td></tr>
</table>

Journal: Here, you can write down your experiences in nature. Think about things that happened, moments that stood out, or how you felt during the walk. Who you were with? What animals or plants did you feel a connection to? Think about sounds and smells. Write freely.

With this section, you'll be able to journal, write down your observations and sketch images. If you have the *Seek* app, use it to help Identify species.

<table>
<tr><td>Draw an image of something you see</td><td>List the things you see on your walk:</td></tr>
</table>

Journal: Here, you can write down your experiences in nature. Think about things that happened, moments that stood out, or how you felt during the walk. Who you were with? What animals or plants did you feel a connection to? Think about sounds and smells. Write freely.

With this section, you'll be able to journal, write down your observations and sketch images. If you have the *Seek* app, use it to help Identify species.

| Draw an image of something you see | List the things you see on your walk: |

Journal: Here, you can write down your experiences in nature. Think about things that happened, moments that stood out, or how you felt during the walk. Who you were with? What animals or plants did you feel a connection to? Think about sounds and smells. Write freely.

With this section, you'll be able to journal, write down your observations and sketch images. If you have the *Seek* app, use it to help Identify species.

Draw an image of something you see

List the things you see on your walk:

Journal: Here, you can write down your experiences in nature. Think about things that happened, moments that stood out, or how you felt during the walk. Who you were with? What animals or plants did you feel a connection to? Think about sounds and smells. Write freely.

With this section, you'll be able to journal, write down your observations and sketch images. If you have the *Seek* app, use it to help Identify species.

Draw an image of something you see

List the things you see on your walk:

____

____

____

____

____

____

____

____

____

Journal: Here, you can write down your experiences in nature. Think about things that happened, moments that stood out, or how you felt during the walk. Who you were with? What animals or plants did you feel a connection to? Think about sounds and smells. Write freely.

With this section, you'll be able to journal, write down your observations and sketch images. If you have the *Seek* app, use it to help Identify species.

<table>
<tr><td>

Draw an image of something you see

</td><td>

List the things you see on your walk:

____

____

____

____

____

____

____

____

____

____

</td></tr>
</table>

Journal: Here, you can write down your experiences in nature. Think about things that happened, moments that stood out, or how you felt during the walk. Who you were with? What animals or plants did you feel a connection to? Think about sounds and smells. Write freely.

With this section, you'll be able to journal, write down your observations and sketch images. If you have the *Seek* app, use it to help Identify species.

<table>
<tr><td>

Draw an image of something you see

</td><td>

List the things you see on your walk:

____

____

____

____

____

____

____

____

____

</td></tr>
</table>

Journal: Here, you can write down your experiences in nature. Think about things that happened, moments that stcod out, or how you felt during the walk. Who you were with? What animals or plants did you feel a connection to? Think about sounds and smells. Write freely.

____
____
____
____
____
____
____
____
____
____
____
____
____

With this section, you'll be able to journal, write down your observations and sketch images. If you have the *Seek* app, use it to help Identify species.

Draw an image of something you see

List the things you see on your walk:

Journal: Here, you can write down your experiences in nature. Think about things that happened, moments that stood out, or how you felt during the walk. Who you were with? What animals or plants did you feel a connection to? Think about sounds and smells. Write freely.

With this section, you'll be able to journal, write down your observations and sketch images. If you have the *Seek* app, use it to help Identify species.

Draw an image of something you see

List the things you see on your walk:

____

____

____

____

____

____

____

____

____

Journal: Here, you can write down your experiences in nature. Think about things that happened, moments that stood out, or how you felt during the walk. Who you were with? What animals or plants did you feel a connection to? Think about sounds and smells. Write freely.

With this section, you'll be able to journal, write down your observations and sketch images. If you have the *Seek* app, use it to help Identify species.

Draw an image of something you see

List the things you see on your walk:

Journal: Here, you can write down your experiences in nature. Think about things that happened, moments that stood out, or how you felt during the walk. Who you were with? What animals or plants did you feel a connection to? Think about sounds and smells. Write freely.

With this section, you'll be able to journal, write down your observations and sketch images. If you have the *Seek* app, use it to help Identify species.

Draw an image of something you see

List the things you see on your walk:

____

____

____

____

____

____

____

____

____

Journal: Here, you can write down your experiences in nature. Think about things that happened, moments that stood out, or how you felt during the walk. Who you were with? What animals or plants did you feel a connection to? Think about sounds and smells. Write freely.

____
____
____
____
____
____
____
____
____
____
____
____
____
____
____

With this section, you'll be able to journal, write down your observations and sketch images. If you have the *Seek* app, use it to help Identify species.

<table>
<tr><td>

Draw an image of something you see

</td><td>

List the things you see on your walk:

</td></tr>
</table>

Journal: Here, you can write down your experiences in nature. Think about things that happened, moments that stood out, or how you felt during the walk. Who you were with? What animals or plants did you feel a connection to? Think about sounds and smells. Write freely.

With this section, you'll be able to journal, write down your observations and sketch images. If you have the *Seek* app, use it to help Identify species.

<table>
<tr><td>

Draw an image of something you see

</td><td>

List the things you see on your walk:

____

____

____

____

____

____

____

____

____

</td></tr>
</table>

Journal: Here, you can write down your experiences in nature. Think about things that happened, moments that stood out, or how you felt during the walk. Who you were with? What animals or plants did you feel a connection to? Think about sounds and smells. Write freely.

With this section, you'll be able to journal, write down your observations and sketch images. If you have the *Seek* app, use it to help Identify species.

<table>
<tr><td>Draw an image of something you see</td><td>List the things you see on your walk:</td></tr>
</table>

Journal: Here, you can write down your experiences in nature. Think about things that happened, moments that stood out, or how you felt during the walk. Who you were with? What animals or plants did you feel a connection to? Think about sounds and smells. Write freely.

With this section, you'll be able to journal, write down your observations and sketch images. If you have the *Seek* app, use it to help Identify species.

Draw an image of something you see

List the things you see on your walk:

Journal: Here, you can write down your experiences in nature. Think about things that happened, moments that stood out, or how you felt during the walk. Who you were with? What animals or plants did you feel a connection to? Think about sounds and smells. Write freely.

With this section, you'll be able to journal, write down your observations and sketch images. If you have the *Seek* app, use it to help Identify species.

<table>
<tr><td>Draw an image of something you see</td><td>List the things you see on your walk:</td></tr>
</table>

Journal: Here, you can write down your experiences in nature. Think about things that happened, moments that stood out, or how you felt during the walk. Who you were with? What animals or plants did you feel a connection to? Think about sounds and smells. Write freely.

With this section, you'll be able to journal, write down your observations and sketch images. If you have the *Seek* app, use it to help Identify species.

<table>
<tr><td>

Draw an image of something you see

</td><td>

List the things you see on your walk:

</td></tr>
</table>

Journal: Here, you can write down your experiences in nature. Think about things that happened, moments that stood out, or how you felt during the walk. Who you were with? What animals or plants did you feel a connection to? Think about sounds and smells. Write freely.

With this section, you'll be able to journal, write down your observations and sketch images. If you have the *Seek* app, use it to help Identify species.

<table>
<tr><td>

Draw an image of something you see

</td><td>

List the things you see on your walk:

</td></tr>
</table>

Journal: Here, you can write down your experiences in nature. Think about things that happened, moments that stood out, or how you felt during the walk. Who you were with? What animals or plants did you feel a connection to? Think about sounds and smells. Write freely.

With this section, you'll be able to journal, write down your observations and sketch images. If you have the *Seek* app, use it to help Identify species.

<table>
<tr><td>Draw an image of something you see</td><td>List the things you see on your walk:</td></tr>
</table>

Journal: Here, you can write down your experiences in nature. Think about things that happened, moments that stood out, or how you felt during the walk. Who you were with? What animals or plants did you feel a connection to? Think about sounds and smells. Write freely.

With this section, you'll be able to journal, write down your observations and sketch images. If you have the *Seek* app, use it to help Identify species.

Draw an image of something you see

List the things you see on your walk:

Journal: Here, you can write down your experiences in nature. Think about things that happened, moments that stood out, or how you felt during the walk. Who you were with? What animals or plants did you feel a connection to? Think about sounds and smells. Write freely.

With this section, you'll be able to journal, write down your observations and sketch images. If you have the *Seek* app, use it to help Identify species.

<table>
<tr><td>Draw an image of something you see</td><td>List the things you see on your walk:</td></tr>
</table>

Journal: Here, you can write down your experiences in nature. Think about things that happened, moments that stood out, or how you felt during the walk. Who you were with? What animals or plants did you feel a connection to? Think about sounds and smells. Write freely.

With this section, you'll be able to journal, write down your observations and sketch images. If you have the *Seek* app, use it to help Identify species.

<table>
<tr><td>

Draw an image of something you see

</td><td>

List the things you see on your walk:

____

____

____

____

____

____

____

____

____

____

</td></tr>
</table>

Journal: Here, you can write down your experiences in nature. Think about things that happened, moments that stood out, or how you felt during the walk. Who you were with? What animals or plants did you feel a connection to? Think about sounds and smells. Write freely.

With this section, you'll be able to journal, write down your observations and sketch images. If you have the *Seek* app, use it to help Identify species.

<table>
<tr><td>

Draw an image of something you see

</td><td>

List the things you see on your walk:

</td></tr>
</table>

Journal: Here, you can write down your experiences in nature. Think about things that happened, moments that stood out, or how you felt during the walk. Who you were with? What animals or plants did you feel a connection to? Think about sounds and smells. Write freely.

With this section, you'll be able to journal, write down your observations and sketch images. If you have the *Seek* app, use it to help Identify species.

<table>
<tr><td>Draw an image of something you see</td><td>List the things you see on your walk:</td></tr>
</table>

Journal: Here, you can write down your experiences in nature. Think about things that happened, moments that stood out, or how you felt during the walk. Who you were with? What animals or plants did you feel a connection to? Think about sounds and smells. Write freely.

With this section, you'll be able to journal, write down your observations and sketch images. If you have the *Seek* app, use it to help Identify species.

Draw an image of something you see

List the things you see on your walk:

Journal: Here, you can write down your experiences in nature. Think about things that happened, moments that stood out, or how you felt during the walk. Who you were with? What animals or plants did you feel a connection to? Think about sounds and smells. Write freely.

With this section, you'll be able to journal, write down your observations and sketch images. If you have the *Seek* app, use it to help Identify species.

<table>
<tr><td>Draw an image of something you see</td><td>List the things you see on your walk:</td></tr>
</table>

Journal: Here, you can write down your experiences in nature. Think about things that happened, moments that stood out, or how you felt during the walk. Who you were with? What animals or plants did you feel a connection to? Think about sounds and smells. Write freely.

With this section, you'll be able to journal, write down your observations and sketch images. If you have the *Seek* app, use it to help Identify species.

<table>
<tr><td>

Draw an image of something you see

</td><td>

List the things you see on your walk:

</td></tr>
</table>

Journal: Here, you can write down your experiences in nature. Think about things that happened, moments that stood out, or how you felt during the walk. Who you were with? What animals or plants did you feel a connection to? Think about sounds and smells. Write freely.

With this section, you'll be able to journal, write down your observations and sketch images. If you have the *Seek* app, use it to help Identify species.

<table>
<tr><td>

Draw an image of something you see

</td><td>

List the things you see on your walk:

</td></tr>
</table>

Journal: Here, you can write down your experiences in nature. Think about things that happened, moments that stood out, or how you felt during the walk. Who you were with? What animals or plants did you feel a connection to? Think about sounds and smells. Write freely.

With this section, you'll be able to journal, write down your observations and sketch images. If you have the *Seek* app, use it to help Identify species.

Draw an image of something you see

List the things you see on your walk:

____

____

____

____

____

____

____

____

____

Journal: Here, you can write down your experiences in nature. Think about things that happened, moments that stood out, or how you felt during the walk. Who you were with? What animals or plants did you feel a connection to? Think about sounds and smells. Write freely.

With this section, you'll be able to journal, write down your observations and sketch images. If you have the *Seek* app, use it to help Identify species.

<table>
<tr><td>

Draw an image of something you see

</td><td>

List the things you see on your walk:

</td></tr>
</table>

Journal: Here, you can write down your experiences in nature. Think about things that happened, moments that stood out, or how you felt during the walk. Who you were with? What animals or plants did you feel a connection to? Think about sounds and smells. Write freely.

With this section, you'll be able to journal, write down your observations and sketch images. If you have the *Seek* app, use it to help Identify species.

Draw an image of something you see

List the things you see on your walk:

Journal: Here, you can write down your experiences in nature. Think about things that happened, moments that stood out, or how you felt during the walk. Who you were with? What animals or plants did you feel a connection to? Think about sounds and smells. Write freely.

With this section, you'll be able to journal, write down your observations and sketch images. If you have the *Seek* app, use it to help Identify species.

Draw an image of something you see

List the things you see on your walk:

Journal: Here, you can write down your experiences in nature. Think about things that happened, moments that stood out, or how you felt during the walk. Who you were with? What animals or plants did you feel a connection to? Think about sounds and smells. Write freely.

The Carpenter Bee

XYLOCOPINAE

The Carpenter Bee

Carpenter bees can be found on every continent except Antartica, and are called Carpenter bees because they are known for making their nests in wood. Carpenter bees do not live in colonies like honey bees. They live alone in nests and hibernate during the winter. The bees aren't really aggressive. Males can be aggressive when being protective of their nest, but only the female carpenter bee has a stinger and rarely is it used. They live in tunnels about an 6 inches deep but sizes may vary.

POLLINATING
Carpenter bees are important pollinators

CLEANING
Bee tongues are called proboscis and they often clean pollen off them

FLIGHT
Male carpenter bees often hover in place.

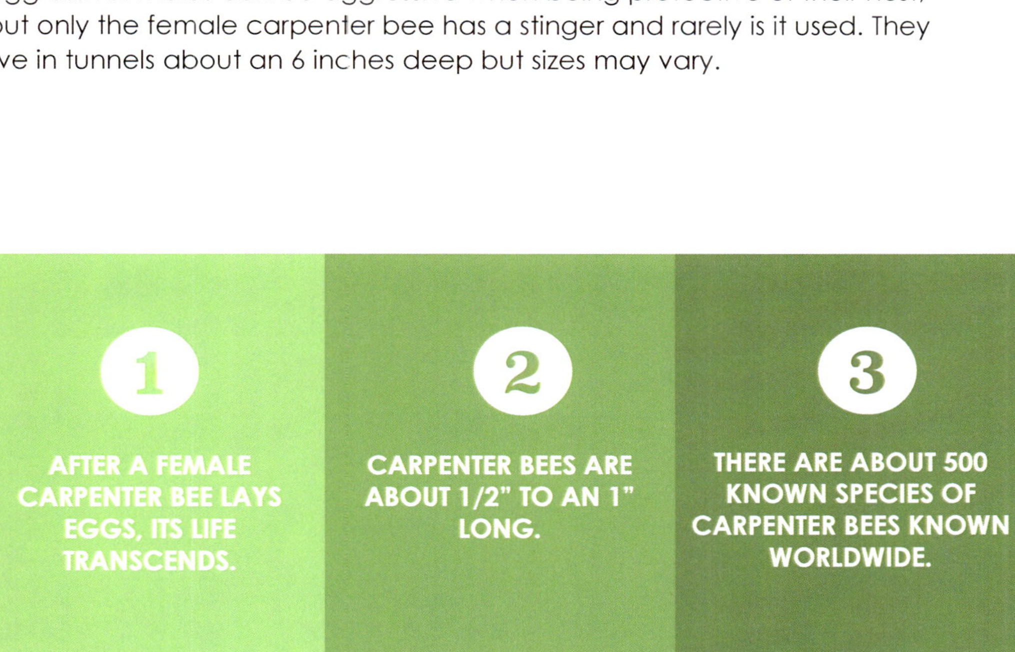

1

AFTER A FEMALE CARPENTER BEE LAYS EGGS, ITS LIFE TRANSCENDS.

2

CARPENTER BEES ARE ABOUT 1/2" TO AN 1" LONG.

3

THERE ARE ABOUT 500 KNOWN SPECIES OF CARPENTER BEES KNOWN WORLDWIDE.

With over 500 types of carpenter bee world-wide, there's a lot to discover. There are two types used on this fact sheet that are commonly found here in Louisiana. The photos were taken at Bayou Sauvage, The Louisiana Nature Center, and City Park in New Orleans.

- Southern Carpenter Bee (Xylocopa Micans)

- Eastern Carpenter Bee (Xylocopa Virginia)

Carpenter Bees not found in Louisiana:

- California Carpenter Bee (Xylocopa californica)

- Valley Carpenter Bee (Xylocopa varipuncta)

- Western Carpenter Bee (Xylocopa occidentalis)

- Large Carpenter Bee (Xylocopa latipes)

- Japanese Carpenter Bee (Xylocopa appendiculata)

- Indian Carpenter Bee (Xylocopa tranquebarica)

- Black Carpenter Bee (Xylocopa violacea)

- Southeast Asian Carpenter Bee (Xylocopa aestuans)

Whenever I see carpenter bees I get happy. To me they are symbols of joy. They can be seen flying from flower to flower helping with pollination. It reminds me of fertility and abundance. They are solitary animals and to live alone symbolizes independence and freedom to create. Whenever I see one in the wild, I'm reminded of these symbols and apply them to my life - John Lacarbiere III

The American Alligator

Alligator mississippiensis

The American Alligator

The American alligator is a large reptile species that is native to the southeastern United States; including states such as Florida, Georgia, Louisiana, Texas, Alabama, and Mississippi. It is one of two living species of alligator, the other being the Chinese alligator (Alligator sinensis). Alligators are primarily solitary animals; although they can tolerate living in close proximity to each other, especially during the mating season. The alligator was endangered but due to conservation, it was able to recover.

Cold Blooded
Gators are cold blooded, meaning they have to use the energy of the sun to warm their body temperature

Buoyancy
Gators are known for sucking in air and positioning their bodies to float or sink at will.

Lifespan
Gators can live 30-50 years in the wild, sometimes much longer

1

ALLIGATORS BREED IN THE SPRING. MOMS BUILD LARGE MOUNDS FOR NESTS. IT TAKES ABOUT 65 DAYS TO HATCH.

2

THEY ARE PREDATORS THAT EAT FISH, BIRDS, AMPHIBIANS, MAMMALS, & OTHER REPTILES. THEY ALSO EAT DEAD FLESH OF OTHER ANIMALS.

3

THEY CAN BE FOUND IN ANY FRESH WATER INCLUDING RIVERS, SWAMPS, LAKES, PONDS, AND EVEN BRACKISH WATER

More Alligator Facts

- **Size:** Adult males can reach an average length of 11 to 15 feet. Some individuals may grow even larger. Adult females are usually smaller, with an average length of 8 to 10 feet

- **Weight:** Adults can weigh anywhere from 500 to 1,000 pounds, with males being larger and heavier than females.

- **Body Shape:** The American alligator has a heavy and stocky body with a long, rounded snout. Its skin is covered in armored plates called scutes, which provide protection and help it blend in with its environment.

- **Coloration:** Baby alligators have a bright yellow coloration with dark bands on their body, which fades as they mature into a darker, olive-brown or black coloration as adults.

- **Estivation:** In periods of drought or extreme heat, alligators can undergo a state of dormancy called estivation. They bury themselves in mud or vegetation and slow down their metabolism to conserve energy until conditions improve.

- **Adaptations:** Alligators have a special rotating membrane over their eyes to protect them in water, a gland in their mouth to excrete excess salt, and a sensor on their nose that can detect movement.

Alligator Symbolism

When I sit and think about what alligators symbolize to me, the first thing that comes to mind is stillness. Alligators know how to use their energy wisely and much of that comes from being still. The idea of being wise comes to mind, knowing the water and the land for millions of years. The toughness of their skin and force of their bite makes me think about strength and power. Lastly, when I see them, I think about home. - John Lacarbiere III

Black and Turkey Vultures

Coragyps atratus & Cathartes aura

Black and Turkey Vultures

Both black vultures & turkey vultures can be found in Louisiana. Both of these species are often seen floating around in the sky or perching in trees. Black vultures are slightly smaller than turkey vultures and have black feathers, a bald head, and a short, hooked beak. Turkey vultures have dark brown or black feathers, a featherless red head, and a long, hooked beak. Both species are scavengers and feed primarily on dead animals, playing an important role in our ecosystem.

Wingspan
Black vultures have a wing span of about 4-5 ft. Turkey vultures have a wingspan of about 5-6 ft.

Weight
Both black and turkey vultures weigh about 4-5 pounds.

US Protected
Both birds are protected by the Migratory Bird Treaty act, making it illegal to hunt them.

1

BOTH BLACK AND TURKEY VULTURES CAN OFTEN BE SEEN TOGETHER.

2

IN NEW ORLEANS, YOU ARE OFTEN ABLE TO SPOT VULTURES LIVING IN BAYOU SAVAUGE.

3

THEY ARE KNOWN AS MIGRATORY BIRDS BUT CAN BE SEEN LIVING IN PLACES YEAR AROUND AS LONG AS THERE'S FOOD AND SHELTER.

More Black & Turkey Vulture Facts

- Black vultures have been known to occasionally prey on weak or injured animals, as well as raiding bird nests for eggs and chicks.

- Black vultures form long-term pair bonds. They typically lay one or two eggs in a nest made of sticks and lined with leaves.

- Turkey vultures are known for their soaring flight, often seen circling in the sky while searching for food using their keen eyesight.

- Turkey vultures have a unique defense mechanism called "urohidrosis," where they defecate on their legs and feet, which helps to kill harmful bacteria and regulate their body temperature.

- Turkey vultures are solitary birds and do not form large groups like black vultures.

- Black vultures are known to range from the southern and eastern parts of the US to Central and South America While The turkey vulture shares the same range, it also has been seen as far as Canada.

- Turkey vultures do not have vocal calls and communicate primarily through body language and behaviors.

- Black vultures can be seen in forests, grasslands, wetlands, as well as urban areas. Turkey vultures the same as well as deserts.

White Tailed Deer

Odocoileus virginianus

White-Tailed Deer

White-tailed deer are native to North America and are one of the most widespread large mammals in the US and Canada. They are named after the white underside of their tail, which they raise as a warning signal when alarmed. White-tailed deer have a reddish-brown summer coat and a grayish-brown winter coat. Fawns, or baby deer, are born with a spotted coat that helps camouflage them from predators. White-tailed deer have a lifespan of up to 6-14 years in the wild, some longer while in captivity.

Great Senses
White-tailed deer are known for their great sight, hearing, and smell, which protects them from predators.

Speed
White-Tailed deer move at speeds of 40mph, making them really fast animals.

Jumping
White-tailed deer are great jumpers, able to jump 10ft into the air.

1
WHITE-TAILED DEER ARE THE OLDEST LIVING SPECIES OF DEER.

2
THEY EAT LEAVES, GRASS, FRUITS, AND NUTS. THEY HAVE A FOUR CHAMBERED STOMACH TO HELP WITH DIGESTION.

3
WHITE TAILED DEER ARE KNOWN TO BE GOOD SWIMMERS AND CAN SWIM ACROSS RIVERS TO GET TO NEW LAND.

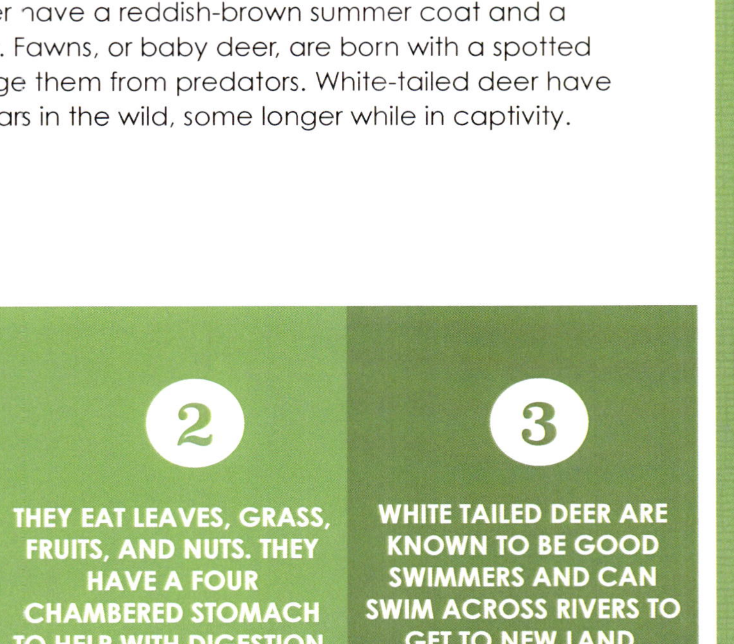

- Adult male white-tailed deer are called bucks, while adult females are called does. Male deer grow antlers, which are shed and regrown each year, while female deer do not have antlers.

- White-tailed deer have a varied social structure. They can be solitary or live in small groups called "yards" or "herds" depending on the season and availability of food.

- White-tailed deer are known for their agility and ability to navigate through various types of terrain, including forests, grasslands, and wetlands. They can easily adapt to different habitats.

- White-tailed deer are crepuscular animals, which means they are most active during dawn and dusk. They are less active during the day and night and tend to rest and ruminate during those times.

- White-tailed deer does are capable of giving birth to one to three fawns per year, typically in the spring or early summer. Fawns are born scentless and are able to stand and walk within hours of birth.

- White-tailed deer populations are managed through hunting. They are important prey animals, providing food for predators such as wolves, cougars, and coyotes. They are also hosts for various parasites, such as ticks and lice.

- During rare times deer are known to eat meat.

Deer Symbolism

Deer remind me of the sunrises and sunsets. You can catch them at dusk or you can catch them at dawn. They remind me of adaptability, being able to adjust to whatever surrounding they're in. They remind me to pay attention to what's around me by using my senses, especially sight and hearing. They remind me of myself, finding comfort alone or with a group. - John Lacarbiere III

Nine-Banded Armadillo

Dasypus novemcinctus

Nine-Banded Armadillo

The nine-banded armadillo is a mammal native to the Americas, ranging from the southern United States to northern Argentina. They are actually not native to Louisiana but can be found all over the state. It is called the "nine-banded" armadillo because it has nine distinct, hinged bands on its back that allow it to curl into a ball for protection. Nine-banded armadillos have a unique appearance with a leathery armor-like shell made of bony plates called scutes, which provide protection from predators.

1

THEY HAVE POOR EYESIGHT BUT AN EXCELLENT SENSE OF SMELL, HEARING, AND TOUCH.

2

THEY ARE PRIMARILY INSECTIVOROUS, FEEDING ON INSECTS, GRUBS, WORMS, AND OTHER SMALL INVERTEBRATES.

3

THEY ARE CAPABLE OF JUMPING 3-4 FEET IN THE AIR WHEN STARTLED, WHICH HELPS THEM ESCAPE FROM PREDATORS.

Living Alone
Each individual typically has its own territory, which it marks with scent glands.

Body Temperature
They have fairly low body temperatures, reaching temps between 32-35 degrees.

Digging
Armadillos are known for their ability to dig with strong forearms and large claws to find food.

More Nine-Banded Armadillo Facts

- Nine-banded armadillos are good swimmers and can hold their breath for up to six minutes. They can cross rivers and creeks by walking along the bottom or swimming across.

- Nine-banded armadillos are known for their reproductive trait of giving birth to identical quadruplets. This is because they always have identical eggs that split into four embryos, resulting in four identical offspring.

- Nine-banded armadillos have a lifespan of about 7-20 years in the wild, depending on various factors such as predation, habitat, and disease.

- Nine-banded armadillos are known for their ability to jump vertically when startled, which is called "jumping jacks" behavior. This behavior is thought to intimidate predators and help the armadillo escape.

- Nine-banded armadillos have a strong sense of smell, which they use to locate food underground, such as insects and other invertebrates.

- Nine-banded armadillos have a flexible diet and can adjust their feeding habits based on food availability, season, and habitat.

- Nine-banded armadillos are capable of consuming large amounts of insects, making them beneficial for controlling insect populations in their habitat.

Armadillo Symbolism

Armadillos remind me of protection. That hard protective shell that they ball into often keeps them safe from predators. They remind me of my childhood self always digging in the dirt in search of bugs, something that always kept me grounded. They live underground as well. Them marking their homes the way they do reminds me of establishing boundaries with others. - John Lacarbiere III

NATURE SCAVENGER HUNT

Try to find as many animals, plants, and shapes as you can. Remember some animals don't like loud noises, so try to keep your voices low and your eyes open. When you find something on the list, mark or check the circle. If you see things that are not on the list, add them to your journal entrees or the blank space on this page. This wou d be a good time to use your "Seek" app.

- O Snail/Slug
- O Anole
- O Blue or green dragonfly
- O Air plant
- O Purple flowers
- O Paper wasp
- O Mushrooms/Fungus
- O Snake

- O Alligator
- O Squirrel
- O Turtles
- O Tiny fish
- O Maple tree
- O Cypress tree
- O Bee
- O Ant
- O Vulture
- O Cardinal
- O Bluejay
- O Frog
- O Grasshopper

NATURE SCAVENGER HUNT

Try to find as many animals, plants, and shapes as you can. Remember some animals don't like loud noises, so try to keep your voices low and your eyes open. When you find something on the list, mark or check the circle. If you see things that are not on the list, add them to your journal entrees or the blank space on this page. This would be a good time to use your "Seek" app.

- ○ Snail/Slug
- ○ Anole
- ○ Blue or green dragonfly
- ○ Air plant
- ○ Purple flowers
- ○ Paper wasp
- ○ Mushrooms/Fungus
- ○ Snake

- ○ Alligator
- ○ Squirrel
- ○ Turtles
- ○ Tiny fish
- ○ Maple tree
- ○ Cypress tree
- ○ Bee
- ○ Ant
- ○ Vulture
- ○ Cardinal
- ○ Bluejay
- ○ Frog
- ○ Grasshopper

NATURE SCAVENGER HUNT

Try to find as many animals, plants, and shapes as you can. Remember some animals don't like loud noises, so try to keep your voices low and your eyes open. When you find something on the list, mark or check the circle. If you see things that are not on the list, add them to your journal entrees or the blank space on this page. This would be a good time to use your "Seek" app.

- ○ Snail/Slug
- ○ Anole
- ○ Blue or green dragonfly
- ○ Air plant
- ○ Purple flowers
- ○ Paper wasp
- ○ Mushrooms/Fungus
- ○ Snake

- ○ Alligator
- ○ Squirrel
- ○ Turtles
- ○ Tiny fish
- ○ Maple tree
- ○ Cypress tree
- ○ Bee
- ○ Ant
- ○ Vulture
- ○ Cardinal
- ○ Bluejay
- ○ Frog
- ○ Grasshopper

NATURE SCAVENGER HUNT

Try to find as many animals, plants, and shapes as you can. Remember some animals don't like loud noises, so try to keep your voices low and your eyes open. When you find something on the list, mark or check the circle. If you see things that are not on the list, add them to your journal entrees or the blank space on this page. This would be a good time to use your "Seek" app.

- ⭕ Snail/Slug
- ⭕ Anole
- ⭕ Blue or green dragonfly
- ⭕ Air plant
- ⭕ Purple flowers
- ⭕ Paper wasp
- ⭕ Mushrooms/Fungus
- ⭕ Snake

- ⭕ Alligator
- ⭕ Squirrel
- ⭕ Turtles
- ⭕ Tiny fish
- ⭕ Maple tree
- ⭕ Cypress tree
- ⭕ Bee
- ⭕ Ant
- ⭕ Vulture
- ⭕ Cardinal
- ⭕ Bluejay
- ⭕ Frog
- ⭕ Grasshopper

SOME PLACES TO VISIT

Here you will find photos of some of the things you might see on trails at the following locations. There are several locations not mentioned and I encourage you to go out and search for more online.

City Park

The Couturie Forest in city Park is a great place to start your journey, but with about 1,300 acres of land starting in Mid City New Orleans, with some estimated 800 year old oak trees, there's lots of life to see. It is also a great place to go bird watching.

Audubon Park

Located in Uptown New Orleans with about 350 acres of land, Audubon park is another place to explore nature. Just across the street from it, you can find The Audubon Zoo and Riverfront or "The Fly."

Audubon Louisiana Nature Center

An 86 acre conservation and education area managed by the Audubon institute. Located in New Orleans East, it has a great boardwalk trail and primitive trail to spot wildlife and fauna. It also has a observatory and interpretive center.

Bayou Sauvage

Bayou Sauvage is a protected National wildlife refuge and is the largest urban wildlife refuge in America. It is Located in New Orleans east, and is about 24,000 acres full of life. There are a few trails to walk here.

Jean Lafitte National Wildlife Park and Barataria Preserve

With over 23,000 acres of Swamps, marshes, and forests, The Barataria preserve is a great place to go exploring wildlife and diverse landscapes. There are several trails to walk. I really love Bayou Coquille trail.

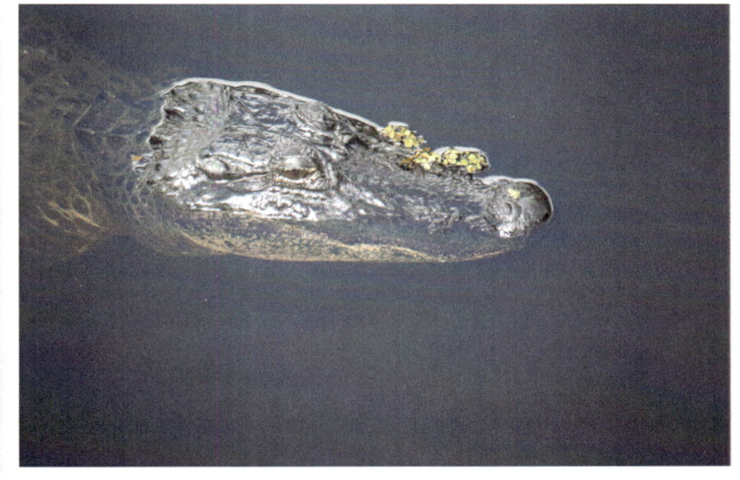

Big Branch Marsh National Wildlife Refuge

Big Branch Marsh is located on the Northshore of Lake Ponchatrain and is about 18,000 acres. A great trail to walk is Boy Scout Rd Trail. Lots of wildlife and plants can be observed at this refuge.

WALK WITH ME

The Journey doesn't have to stop here. If you're local or visiting, schedule a nature walk with me. Bring this book and let s explore wherever you'd like to go in New Orleans or any other Louisiana trail. Remember this book only touches on a few of the natural areas here in Louisiana but it is indeed designed for the entire state. I've pretty much walked every trail there is here in Louisiana and I continually walk and document the changes I see. Or if walking isn't your thing and you'd like to sit and meditate, that's also availab e. Email **jlacarbiere@gmail.com** to schedule your walk and/or meditation.

Other ways to walk with me:

Back to Nature Curriculum: The *Back to Nature Curriculum* is an optional 1-6 week nature course that not only focuses on the natural side of New Orleans and other parts of Louisiana but a course that will aim to give you (and/or your child/children/partner) a better understanding of mindfulness and self. In this course we will explore the various ecosystems here in Louisiana and learn about the wildlife and plant life and how it all connects to how we live. We will also learn things like outdoor cooking, nature photography and farming. In the end we will be able to share basic life skills in nature as well as identify some wildlife and how we can conserve these landscapes for future generations. Space is limited and availability varies. Email **jlacarbiere@gmail.com** to find out more.

John Lacarbiere's Wildlife fact Files: You may have seen this section in the book. It is the start of a optional monthly subscriptior where every month you'll be mailed new fact file sheets to add to your collection. Email **jlacarbiere@gmail.com** to find out more.

Join my Patreon: If you'd like a more intimate glimpse at how I feel when I spend time in nature or see nature photography and gain access to walks, classes, and more, subscribe to **patreon.com/ johnlacarbiereiii**

Follow my nature photography page on instagram: A great way to see what I see on walks and get info on upcoming nature related events follow me on instagram at **instagram.com/jlacarbierephotograhpy**

THANK YOU

Thank you for helping me share this book. I hope that you are inspired. I hope that you too share your love for nature with the world as I intend to continue to. With love - John Lacarbiere III

NOTES